THE
BOOK OF
CATITUDES

Dubious Wit & Wisdom
from Cats

The Book of Catitudes

13-Digit ISBN: 978-1-64643-346-9
10-Digit ISBN: 1-64643-346-7

This book may be ordered by mail from
the publisher. Please include $5.99 for
postage and handling. Please support
your local bookseller first!

Books published by Cider Mill Press
Book Publishers are available at special
discounts for bulk purchases in
the United States by corporations,
institutions, and other organizations.
For more information, please contact
the publisher.

Cider Mill Press Book Publishers
"Where good books are ready for press"
501 Nelson Place
Nashville, Tennessee 37214

cidermillpress.com

Typography: Providence Sans Pro

Printed in Malaysia

23 24 25 26 27 COS 6 5 4 3 2

THE
BOOK OF
CATITUDES

Dubious Wit & Wisdom from Cats

Illustrations by Rhoda Domingo

CIDER MILL
PRESS

BOOK
PUBLISHERS

This is my property now.

Yes, I am judging you.

Psst. I left this just for you.

Only packing the essentials.

You bought this pillow
for me, right?

Let me out! Let me out!
Let me out!

Let me in! Let me in!
Let me in!

Oops.

Talk to the butt.

You shall not pass.

Now it looks better.

This seems like a nice spot. To pee. Where you'll never find it.

Get up. I've prepared a
PowerPoint presentation for
why we should sell the dog.

I brought you a present.

Did someone say catnip?

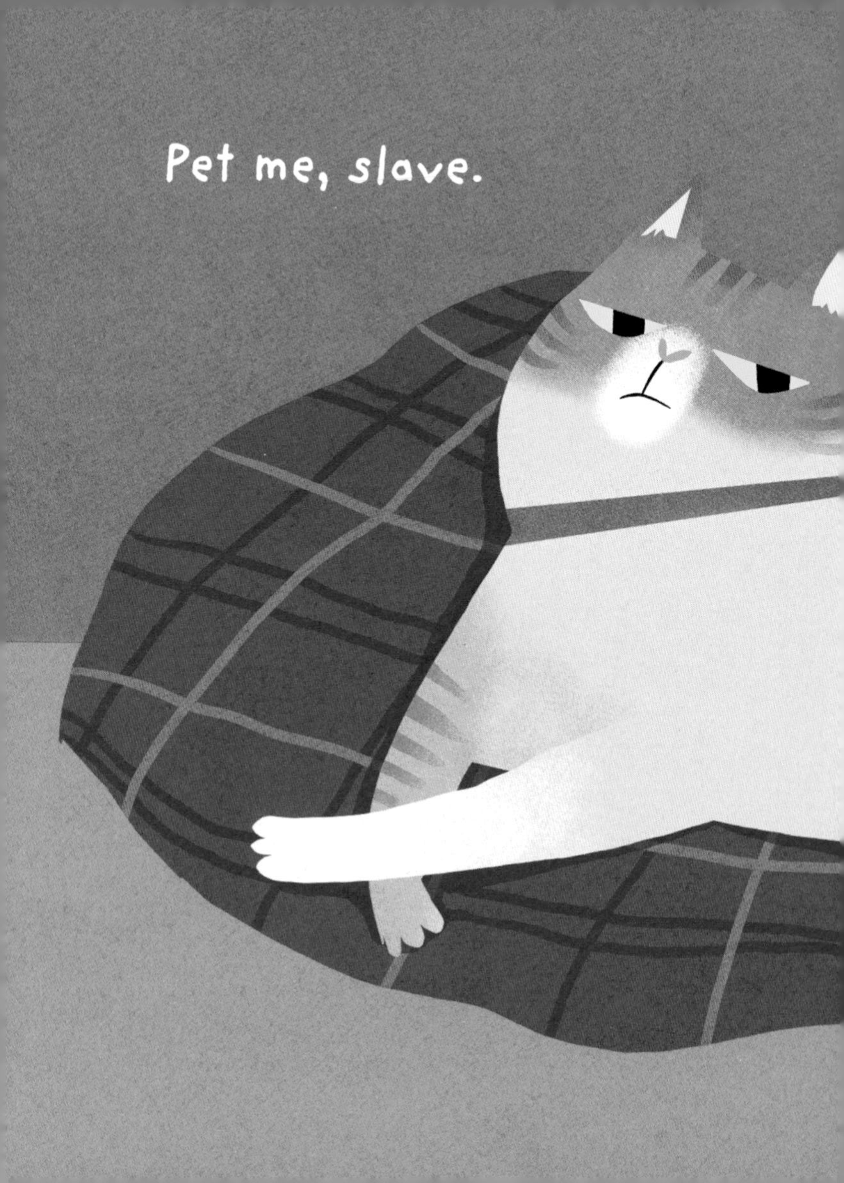
Pet me, slave.

You don't mind sharing,
do you?

These are for me, right?

If I fit, I sit.

Stealth mode activated.

Feet? Attack!

Oh, you thought you could have a moment to yourself?

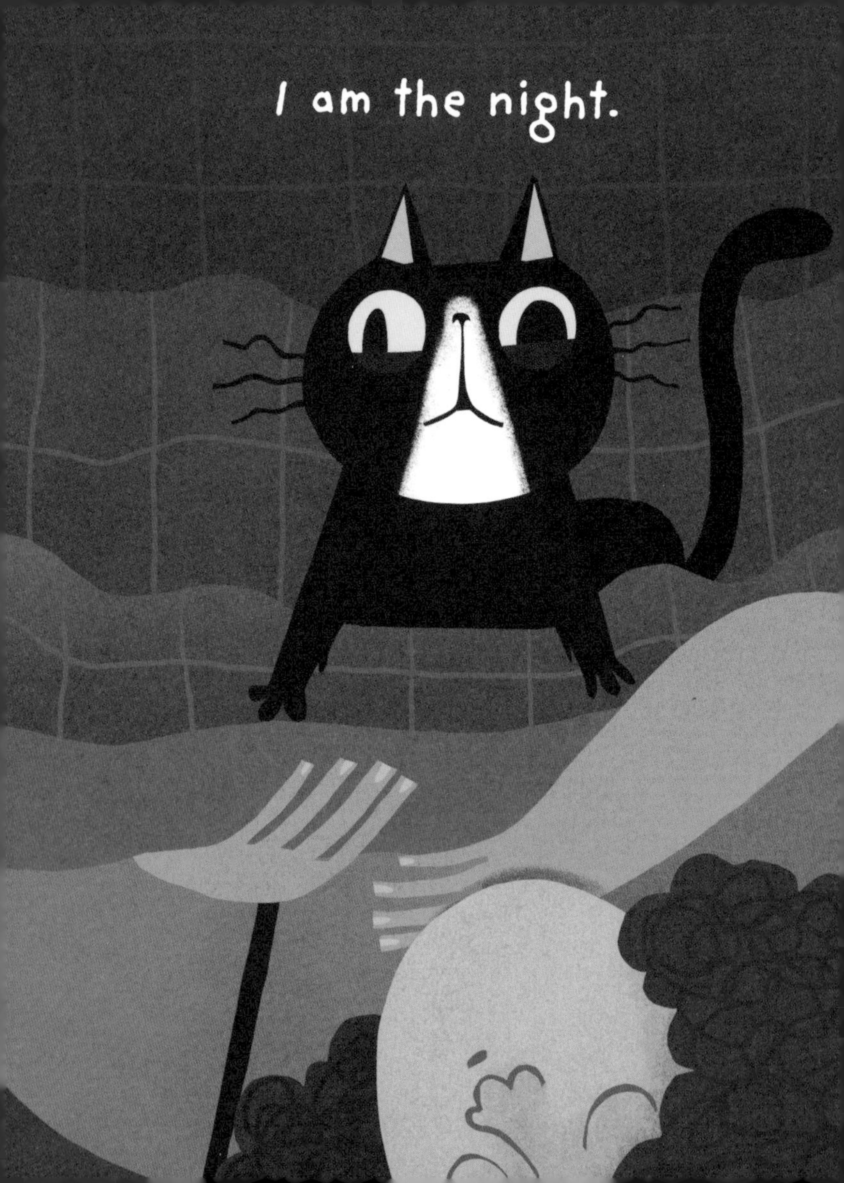
I am the night.

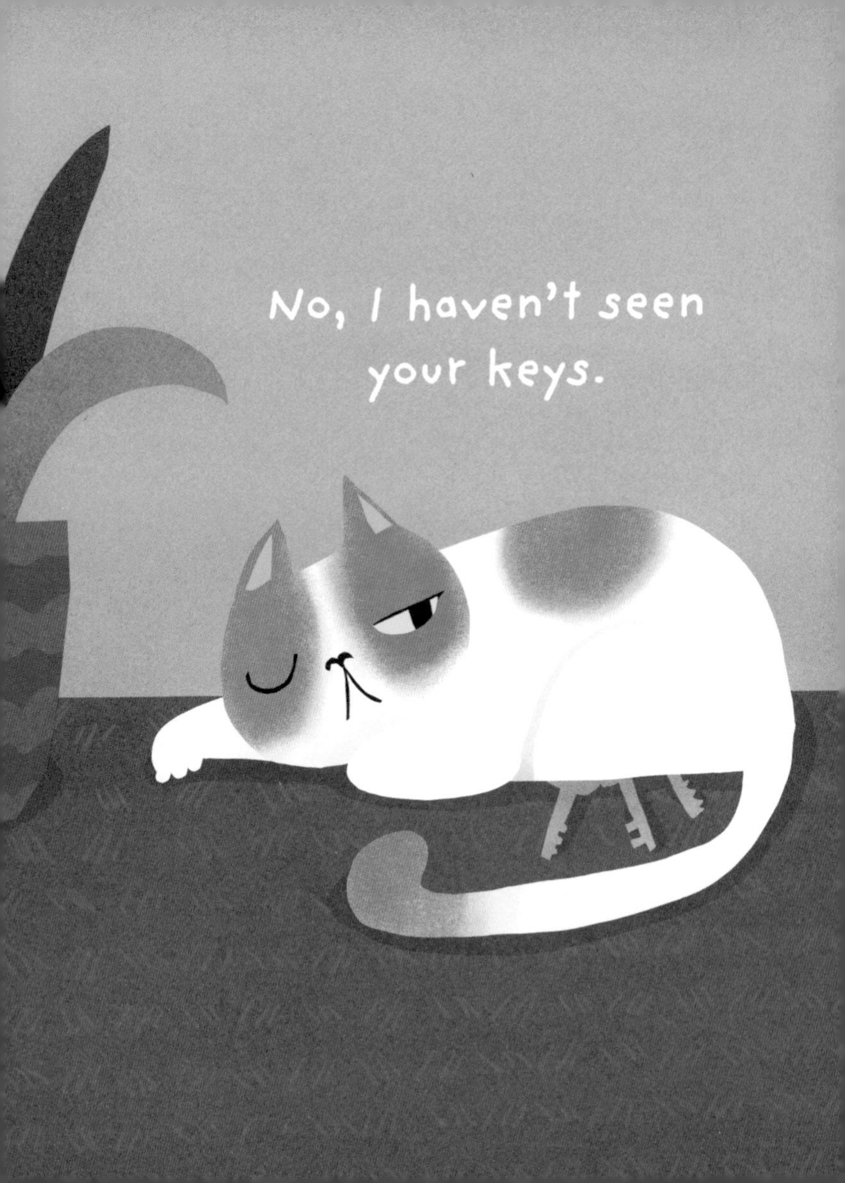
No, I haven't seen
your keys.

My toxic trait is attacking your calves whenever you are carrying something fragile, heavy, and expensive.

This litter box is spill-
proof? Challenge accepted.

I'm going to scratch at
this door until you open it.

Jump scare!

Legs? Do you mean vertical surfaces that I can scale?

You know what would make this carpet even better? If I dragged my butt across it.

Touch my belly and die.

I love you so much that I
barfed on your pillow.

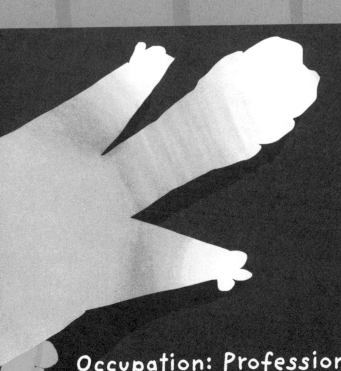

Occupation: Professional
Tripping Hazard

I insist on engaging in a vicious battle with the doorstop at 3 a.m.

A closed door can't stop me.

Yum, did someone say houseplants?

Not a chance. Bad dog.

About Cider Mill Press Book Publishers

Good ideas ripen with time. From seed to harvest,
Cider Mill Press brings fine reading, information,
and entertainment together between the covers of its
creatively crafted books. Our Cider Mill bears fruit twice a
year, publishing a new crop of titles each spring and fall.

CIDER MILL
PRESS

BOOK
PUBLISHERS

"Where Good Books Are Ready for Press"

501 Nelson Place
Nashville, Tennessee 37214

cidermillpress.com